AUTHORITY SELLING™

➤ Opening More Doors to Closing More Business ◆

By: Mike Saunders, MBA

I am an Authority Marketing Strategist and creator of the Authority Selling™ System. I also am the Talk Show Host of "Influential Entrepreneurs on the Business Innovators Radio Network.

Mike Saunders, MBA
Authority Positioning Strategist

As Featured On

My Team helps you build your "Authority Positioning Portfolio™" which will help you become recognized as an Expert in your field through my proprietary 3-Hour Authority™ System. Credibility brings with it great opportunity! From speaking, generating quality referrals, commanding higher fees to closing more sales faster.

Mike Saunders, MBA
Business Strategist | Marketing Fanatic
Mike@MarketingHuddle.com
www.MarketingHuddle.com

Contact Mike to speak at your Organization or Event about Authority Selling™

Table of Contents

Introduction

In this book, you will not find sales scripts or how to overcome objections. There are plenty of other great books that provide solutions to that need. What you will find, is how to build and use a platform of "Authority Positioning" to separate yourself from your competition so that you become the obvious choice.

This book is written in a unique way to immerse yourself in the content through a conversational writing style as if I am speaking right to you. You will also find that you will learn more easily from this book, not only because of the flow of the content, but there is an integrated Authority Selling™ Action Guide which allows you to implement your learning as you go!

Authority Selling™ includes concepts based cutting-edge research by social psychologists and infused with marketing psychology principles of Authority, Social Proof, Scarcity, Repetition, and others. To learn more about these powerful concepts, check out books by Dr. Robert B. Cialdini: "Influence: The Psychology of

Persuasion" and "Pre-Suasion: A Revolutionary Way to Influence and Persuade"; Tom Hopkins: "Master the Art of Selling" or John Di Lemme: "17 Highly Guarded Strategies to Close Every Sale Guaranteed PLUS How to Combat the Fear of Closing"

To separate yourself from your competitors you must stand out. This can take on many different forms, but the most efficient way is to stand out by being a credible Influence and Authority in your field.

As you read this book, I want you to understand the simplicity of the concept of developing your Authority Positioning. This strategy is not meant to make you a national celebrity, but to establish you as the premier brand in your Sphere of Influence and build from there over time.

Based on the NLP concept of Framing, a "Pre-Frame" is a powerful approach that allows you to strategically and subtlety let your target audience know what is going to happen and how they should think about it.

When this is done in advance of them connecting with you, whether days or minutes, you are positioned as a credible Authority.

Think about cold-calling. The person answering your call has no clue you are calling and knows absolutely zero about you, not to mention the fact that they are in the middle of something when you call and are not in the proper frame-of-mind to respond positively to you. How likely are you going to be able to set an appointment or sell your product or service?

AUTHORITY SELLING™ EXECUTION TIP:

If you do want to use phone selling, consider an initial call lasting less than a minute to introduce yourself to them and ask if you can send them some information on how you solve a problem that you know they have. You then can set up a service so that with just a few mouse-clicks a glossy greeting card with your logo, picture and a custom message pre-loaded will be dropped in the mail to them. The message should also include a link to your Authority Positioning Portfolio™, or a short email with links to news media or radio interviews you have done. By doing this, you will enhance your results to give you the highest level of success in phone sales when you call them back the following week and open up a dialogue!

Research conducted by American social psychologist, Stanley Milgram discovered that people trust the people they see as Experts in their Sphere of Influence. The power of this concept is that you can become THE Expert even if you are starting out from scratch, BUT you must know how to leverage your knowledge and expertise to get visible to your target audience.

Consider this: your time is valuable, right? You have such limited time to research your buying decisions, so how do you make them? Don't you look for reviews and testimonials? Don't you want to know that the brand you are looking at is reputable? What if they are the leader in their field? As long as the price is comparable, don't you choose the company that is on top? Sure you do. And so do your prospects!

The "Pre-frame" is not the only concept to consider. Think about after you meet with a prospect, would boosting your Credibility and Authority help them make their decision to select you? When the sale does not happen during the meeting, you run the risk of losing momentum so having a strategically-designed Authority Positioning Portfolio™ to leave with them will increase your chances of closing the sale. Finally, consider post-purchase behavior and "buyer's remorse." Once the deal has been made, if you can consistently provide these assets to your new customer over time, they are assured that they made a wise decision in choosing to work with you.

Using this concept of a strategically created "Authority Positioning Portfolio™," you can see a unique protection in your business to reduce the chance of your competitors from gaining ground. Your prospects do not know what you know about your industry. Period. So when you can "pre-frame and post-frame" your expertise with educational pieces of content from a variety of choices such as radio or podcast interviews, media mentions in news stories or the fact that you are a published author on the exact topic your target audience is in need of solving...you are positioned powerfully!

The great business guru Chet Holmes is famous for saying: "Experts will get three times more referrals as salespeople." Using this approach, you have the unique ability to use this science of setting your prospect's buying behavior.

This is Authority Selling™

Authority Selling™ Strategy:

How to Establish Your Authority Positioning

With Authority Selling™, the very first thing we need to do is establish our Authority Position. What does that mean for you? You cannot just wait around and hope that someone will notice that you're good at whatever you do. Do you realize that when you make decisions, it's based on a lot of psychological triggers? We will cover a few of the most important triggers as you read and implement action steps in this book.

One of the things you need to keep in mind; when the media is talking about you or your business, this gives you instant credibility. Let me say that again. When the media is talking about you or your business, that gives you instant credibility, and why is that? It's because it's a third-party source. Let's think about the chicken and the egg. Do you want to wait and hope that the media might talk about you someday because you've spent years calling yourself an Expert or would you rather have others see you as the Expert right now because the media is talking about you today?

This is a critical piece of Authority Selling™ strategy; there are so many messages coming at us individually each and every day that it's hard for people to tell the difference between what they want to pay attention to and what they should pay attention to. You need to be consistently establishing yourself as an Authority and as an Expert. We're seeing this in today's media and the marketing world; the necessity of your personal brand and building an ongoing personal branding strategy.

I remember years ago going to a seminar called "The Brand of You"; you may be a realtor, financial advisor, anyone in professional services, and you want to brand yourself as the Expert because you might not work for the company you currently are with for your entire career. You want your clientele and your target audience following you. You need be the person that they're trusting, not only the name brand you work for.

Let's define this: "A brand is a set of expectations or stories or expectations that people have of this service you're about to give them based on their past, based on their friends that have made recommendations." When you take all that together, it's a consumer's decision to choose one product or service over another, and that is huge.

What sets you apart from your competition? You absolutely have to be building a brand in your competitive industry. You have to be unique and remarkable, and then you have to be able to share that in your messaging online and offline. Part of this is knowing who you are as a person and as a brand representative of your company; knowing who your target audience is so that you can understand their problems, concerns, and issues and know how to communicate your solution that your company provides to them. This lays the foundation for setting yourself apart from your competition. Your Authority is your position in the mind of the consumer, your target audience. When you can articulate your "why," the reason you are in business and passionate about doing what you do, this becomes your brand.

Authority Positioning is all about becoming an educator and an advocate for your target audience and putting yourself in their shoes and helping them achieve success. When you share value in authentic and unique ways, your prospects and clients begin to take notice. They call you the Expert or Authority and you never have to. Why is that? Because they're so used to other salespeople or competitors in your industry, who are pushing their products and services on them. Now when you come in, and begin educating them on their options and choices so that they become an educated buyer of whatever you are selling, they feel the difference and will respond in a positive way. It has been said in the past, "People don't like to be sold, but they like to buy." Well, how do they make that buying decision? It's by being educated enough to make those choices.

Barbara Corcoran from the Shark Tank has explained how she became the go-to source for real estate in her area. She began to get quoted in popular news media about her real estate predictions and research. Barbara understands the power of the media, and she used it to catapult her business to success. Now remember, you might not get quoted in the big papers immediately. She mentioned Wall Street Journal & New York Times. You may not be able to start off there right away; but in your area, what if you have a local newspaper and you get to know some of the reporters or the editor? What if you give some contributions? What if you get quoted in that newspaper? Well, then maybe that gets out, and you can get quoted in statewide papers. You have to be thinking about this strategy of the "third-party mention" as opposed to you saying how great you are.

Here's a scary thing to keep in mind. If you don't invest in a formal Authority media campaign tailored to meet your unique needs of your target audience, you risk losing market share to well-organized competitors. Let me focus in on this word "invest" because this is an investment, not an expense. When you invest in an Authority Positioning media campaign, it has to be a long-term and consistent investment.

Which one of these two types of personalities has more credibility? Someone that says that they are the Expert in their field or a news media outlet that says that for them? Third party endorsement beats self-imposed titles and slogans every single time. Yes, you need to let people know, and you need to say that you are an Expert in a specific area, but when it's coupled with third party media mentions and endorsements from third party sources, that's when the true power comes in.

Consider this: journalists are out there searching for authorities in a specific vertical. They read news articles and blogs, and if you read their stories, you'll see references to Experts; these are people who are authorities in their niche. They're essential to the media. When a journalist develops a story, they have to get quotations, opinions, facts. They need to connect with people that are in the know.

AUTHORITY SELLING™ EXECUTION TIP:

As you are developing your Authority, remember that you are laying the groundwork and bread-crumbs for not only your prospects to find you, but also journalists who are researching topics to report on! Don't be surprised if you get contacted by a journalist working on a story and asking for you to contribute because they saw you published a book or spoke on a radio show on the topic! You can enhance this by using services such as MuckRack.com to get the attention of journalists who cover your industry

Now the same thing kicks in for them that happens to your prospects…. they are busy and have no extra time, so they choose options at the top of their search. When your solution to a specific problem, or opinions on an industry trend, are seen in their search, guess whose chance of getting contacted just skyrocketed? You!

Then, your chance to get more media exposure increases because it gets much, much easier to get more media mentions when you've already been mentioned in the media. It opens doors to other business-building opportunities like speaking engagements or podcast interviews or radio show interviews.

When you put links to where you've been mentioned in the media on a press or a media page on your website, it creates instant "trust triggers" with your potential clients and prospects who land on your site.

AUTHORITY SELLING™ EXECUTION TIP:

Go to the story and print it as a PDF then upload it to your website to use that URL in your promotions. This way you always have the credibility of being in that media release with the date and time in the story even if the link drops off their site over time.

Here's something you should do right now: Google "ZMOT," which stands for Zero Moment of Truth. It's a free e-book that a former Google employee wrote, and it references back to the old days when you would go into a store, and someone would give you a brochure and then they would say, "Call us if you have any questions." Well, today if you go to a store or a car dealership you go in educated more than most of the salespeople that are working there because you did internet research.

When you can do research upfront, you're going in as an educated buyer, and you're going in knowing the direction that you want to go with that product or that service. The old moment of truth was when they would buy the product and see if it worked. Now the "zero moment of truth" is when someone goes online and starts doing some initial preliminary research on that product. If they're looking for best Dallas, Texas chiropractor, the moment of truth used to be when they would go to the chiropractor and get the first session and see how they liked it. Now the zero moment of truth is when they Google that phrase and they start seeing all of the different listings that come up, all of the competitors, all of the things that are said about the local area chiropractors, the reviews, the social proof. They formulate their opinions based on what they research and choose the one that has the most Authority and trust. Period.

Knowing that journalists are searching for authorities in their niche to write stories about, and knowing that prospects are looking for solutions to their problem, you need to be putting out content that is educational in a way that advocates for your prospect's success and solves a problem that they may have.

Let's use the chiropractor as the example. Do you have a pain in your knee after running? Maybe this chiropractor would write a blog post on this, or maybe they were interviewed on a podcast or a radio show that they get out there online. When someone is Googling a phrase such as "why do my knees hurt after running?" and Google sees from their IP address that they're in the local area, chances are pretty good that this local Dallas chiropractor interview on knee pain and how to eliminate it will show up.

The prospect is thinking, "Yeah, that's my question!" If it was YOU, that put out that content, they click on it, and they listen to that interview. You then are the Authority because your competitors aren't doing this. What you need to have developed is a whole list of "Frequently Asked" questions and a whole list of "Should-Ask" questions. Your target audience has a lot of questions that typically come up, "Frequently Asked" questions. Answer those with two, three, four paragraphs for each one. Then write another list of ten "Should-Ask" questions. If a prospective patient or client or customer of yours, were to ask these questions they would really to the heart of the matter, the "Should-Ask" questions…. they don't even know enough to ask these questions, but if they did, these are really, magnificent questions. Now you have 10 "Frequently Asked" questions and 10 "Should-Ask" questions, and you've answered them.

Could you write a blog post about each one easily? Could you get interviewed on a radio show or a podcast on a few easily? Now all of these breadcrumbs are getting out there online and the journalists that are searching for these types of things, whatever your industry, they stumble across that and maybe they're contacting you for a comment to get mentioned in their story they are researching. Maybe it's the prospective patient; so all of this educational content is building your credibility and Authority.

Research shows that when someone hears about a business or entrepreneur, over 85% of the time, they will go directly to Google and search for the owner's name and the name of the business. They want to see what is being said online about them; from reviews to news stories or just online presence. When you begin accumulating the media mentions, radio/podcast interviews and books published, you need to keep a collection of these URL's and add to your SEO strategy! Think about it, Amazon is a credible platform, so when you have a book published on Amazon and the URL to the book is inserted in your SEO campaigns for your brand name and primary keywords, what do you think will show up in the top Google results?

Let's say that you have laid the groundwork, and get mentioned in the media or interviewed by a reporter, and that's wonderful. Now you use that. You've got a piece of content which can be accumulated into your Authority Positioning Portfolio™. As each and every one of these assets are being created, get a copy of it. When you're interviewed on a podcast, get a recording of that.

Now all of a sudden, you're building this vast, ever-expanding portfolio of your Authority and Expertise, but you cannot just do it one time. Just being seen on another site, a media site is not enough to establish the level of Authority you're going to need to be recognized as the foremost Authority in your area. You have to create a pattern that involves extending your reach both online and offline that leads to more Influence with your prospects. You need to be consistently quoted in news stories, maybe mentioned in a press release, be interviewed on a radio show or a podcast, be featured in a business magazine, writing a book. Constantly getting in front of your target audience and your strategic alliances so that they are seeing all the things that you're doing out there.

Once you start getting these Authority Positioning assets in place, you need to be proactive in getting the word out and promoting your Influence and Authority in your marketing. I like to call them "humble brags," you don't want to be prideful and obnoxious about it, but just casually mention to your e-mail list or your blog readers or your social media platforms that you were featured in a press release or a recent interview or publishing project. This creates bursts of credibility that attract the right attention; you will be found quickly when your prospects are ready to take action because you posted this "humble brag." Here's an example: "Hey, it was such an honor to be interviewed on such-and-such a podcast. Here's the recording. Let me know what you think!"

Send that to your e-mail list and post to your social media platforms (consistently as they happen). Well, someone out there in your network might forward that to a friend of theirs, and now you're the Expert because you were interviewed. You have compelling Positioning happening for your brand which goes beyond your 1st-level network. This is laying the groundwork for the Authority Selling™ process.

The great business guru Chet Holmes was famous for saying: "Experts will get three times more referrals as salespeople." Because people don't like to be sold, but they like to buy, and they want to buy from someone they trust who is an Expert or an Authority. It becomes so much easier to get quality referrals when your network can point to your accomplishments.

Once you've started getting your message out there through interviews or press releases or media mentions, look at publishing your book. Now you may be thinking that you can never do that because maybe you have this feeling that you can't even write a blog post or an e-mail much less a book!

I agree that it's very daunting to think about writing a book. I have said for quite a while that there seems to be a "disconnect" between your head and your hands, whether you hold a pen in your hands to write or your hands on the keyboard to type a book, there seems to be a disconnect! Am I right? You've got all this knowledge and expertise in your head, but you can't get it out.

I've got a process called "3-Hour Authority™" where it only takes three hours of your time, and you will become an Amazon best-selling author without writing a word including a full Authority Positioning Portfolio™ built out for you. It's a really, really unique process, and if you would like more information, you can learn more at www.3HourAuthority.com

Here are a few benefits of being a published author:

- You become a credible Expert practically overnight.

- You become a celebrity in your niche. People associate "published author" with "Expert."

- It opens up media opportunities, when reporters are looking for credible Experts on the topic they need to write their story on, if they're Googling around and they see that you wrote a book on just such a topic, maybe they're contacting you over someone else that just wrote a blog post.

- It opens up speaking opportunities. When you can speak in front of an audience such as your local chamber of commerce, Rotary club, or an association that you're a member of, you then become quite the Expert because you're the person on stage. It becomes so easy to get that speaking engagement because you're an Amazon best-selling author.

• Your sales cycle is dramatically shortened. With Authority Selling™, a salesperson goes in trying to push someone to close the sale right away. You already have this pre-frame in the prospects' mind that you're an Expert and Authority. You were mentioned in the media. You were interviewed on a podcast.

Does it guarantee you one hundred percent close rate? No, but if you currently close five out of ten appointments, maybe it gets you to seven out of ten. It's a dramatic increase in profit with the same amount of work being seen as an Authority and Expert.

Remember, you're not going to get paid much in royalties from the book being written, but you're going to get paid because you wrote the book. With these doors that are open, selling more of your product, selling more of your services, getting consulting. It doesn't matter what industry that you're in, you can become an Authority and get more business when you have some of these Authority Positioning assets working for you.

I met with a client recently, and she had this 8-1/2 x 11 full-color, glossy, six-page brochure that she handed me about her business. I asked her how much that cost, and she said, it costs her $6.50 to print each one of those. Well, I showed her a copy of an Amazon book, 120 pages, glossy cover, the author's name on the cover and the author's picture on the back.

I said, "This book cost about $2.75 plus about $2 in shipping…so for $4.75 you're handing a prospect a BOOK! Imagine the amplified impact of handing your prospect your book, compared to a glossy brochure!"

Something else to consider is micro-specialization. It's a super powerful strategy to become the perfect solution to your prospect's particular problem.... not every problem they may have! Narrowing in on just one of the problems your prospect has and providing a solution, is 10X more effective than trying to tell everything about what you do and attempting to be all things to all people.

As an example, if you're a realtor, you could say, "I help people buy and sell homes. That's way too broad. You could say, "I help real estate investors find, fix, and flip properties in the Phoenix, Arizona, market." Very, very specific.

If you're a chiropractor: "I help people that are in pain." Too broad. You could say, "I help automobile accident victims recover from whiplash quickly without long-lasting effects. Micro-Specialization helps you laser-target your best prospects and turn them into customers.

Keep Micro-specialization in mind when you're beginning to develop your Authority Positioning Portfolio™ so that your Authority Selling™ strategy is a success. Now when you think about the one solution to your target audience's problem, you may have three, four or five solutions. If you're that chiropractor, you might work with more than just car accident victims. After you've developed a portfolio of your media mentions and interviews and book, you just start the process over again and start focusing on your solution to a new problem. So maybe that chiropractor now is talking about injuries at work or it might be helping with maternity care, things like that. If you're a realtor, maybe you're talking about first-time home buyers.

You want to have that very specific micro-specialization so that you can attract the right prospects directly to you like a magnet.

AUTHORITY SELLING™ ACTION GUIDE:

Make a list of your key values, your passions, the ways that you do business that are different than what your competitors are doing in your industry. Focus on your "Why" and Vision.

_____

_____

_____

_____

_____

_____

_____

_____

_____

_____

_____

_____

_____

_____

_____

_____

_____

_____

_____

_____

_____

_____

_____

_____

_____

_____

_____

_____

_____

_____

_____

_____

Authority Selling™ Strategy:

Understanding the Psychology of Marketing.

How to ethically persuade people to buy from you.

The idea of using psychology as a way to persuade customers to buy from you seems a bit forceful or shady to many people. They hate the idea that they may be manipulating customers in an unethical way. Much of that thinking stems from traditional tactics used by unscrupulous advertisers. There are still salespeople who think they can use secret tricks to get people to make a purchasing decision. In reality, any tricks will hurt your business in the long run and will not build the type of long-lasting relationships that are the foundation of successful businesses. The truth is, psychology is just a science that helps you understand how your customers are thinking. When you can connect with your target market on a deeper level emotionally, you will be able to reach them and help them a lot better than trying to use any tricks.

If you can connect with your audience on a deeper level to understand what your customers are thinking at each stage of the buying process, then you can provide the information that they need which leads to a buying decision. Think of what we were talking about in the previous chapter with educating and becoming an advocate for your customers' success. If you can understand what your customers are thinking at a particular stage, and then educate them at that stage, they're more likely to continue to the next stage with you in the buying process. Even more important, you'll learn how to use psychology in an ethical way.

If you have a good grasp of basic psychology, you can figure out how to effectively communicate how your product meets your target audiences' needs. When you can connect with your customers on an emotional level, you can grab their attention in a way that any dry, unemotional marketing could never achieve.

OK let's get started, we need to start with an overview of the major theories of psychology, and many have pointed to Maslow's Hierarchy of Needs. Abraham Maslow developed this theory of the levels that people will go through. His theory centers on a hierarchy of needs. When you think of each of these levels in light of Authority Selling™, you can see the huge opportunity.

Maslow's theory states that each of us achieves needs by starting at the bottom of the hierarchy and working our way up. Only when the lowest needs are met can we move to the next level. If the need isn't met, the person focuses on fulfilling that need before they can concentrate on the next step. Each person is motivated to move from the bottom to the top. It's important for marketers because it defines people's different motivations. As a marketer, we need to fully understand our customers and their motivations when it comes to choosing and buying products. From the perspective of developing our Authority Positioning, and using that in our sales process to move people through these levels, it now becomes easier because of the leverage which credibility provides.

The first level is the physiological need. These are biological or physical needs without which you might experience pain. Air, food, water, shelter, warmth and sleep. You may be providing solutions to these types of needs such as air purification, organic food, water purifiers, etc. You need to show people that this is an essential need and appeal to them at that level. When you layer in your Authority in that industry, by showing them where you've been quoted or having some teachings in an article, being interviewed on a podcast, or mentioned in the media, now people begin to trust you on a deeper level.

The next level is safety need. Safety ranges from basics such as protection from the elements or immediate danger. On the personal level, these needs revolve around the core need for stability and freedom from fear; without which we would be consumed by anxiety. Let's think about this about selling. When you can talk about the features that protect the prospective customer and their family, now you can appeal to them from a safety standpoint which resonates with them at this deep level.

The next level is the social need. This involves love, belonging, feeling socially accepted; specific needs at this stage may be a sense of belonging to a community or having friends, functioning well in social situations and having romantic relationships. Being accepted is a very strong driver, and in the selling process, it can be used as a way to connect deeper with your target audience. What if we were looking at a product or service and once we bought it, we were told that we would be included in a private Facebook group for all the users of this group to brainstorm and mastermind and collaborate? Would you like to learn from other users about how they're using the product most effectively? I am a member of a few of these types of groups, and I know that there is tremendous power in that.

This ties-in to the sense of belonging because as a member of this group, you are getting those needs met. Also, many times the group leader has created a unique name for their followers; there's that extra sense of belonging and connection.

Maslow's next level is esteem. At this level, they're associating with appreciation and respect. Once our psychological needs, safety needs, and social needs are met, we begin to focus on personal worth. This area includes achievement, mastery, independence, prestige, self-respect, and respect from others. This integrates very well with Authority Positioning because your prospects want to feel special and respected. They want to do business with someone who appreciates them. People want to brag about the person they're doing business with. They may say, "Oh I do business with so and so. They're a published author…or they were just seen on the local news interviewed about___."

The esteem needs level is a very powerful driver when we're talking about Authority Positioning and Authority Selling™.

AUTHORITY SELLING™ EXECUTION TIP:

In building your Authority Positioning assets, focus on a few of these areas so that you can use them in your sales process. For example, in a radio interview, you can appeal to the listener's Esteem by talking about how your brand and service packages are high-end and that you are extremely selective regarding the clients you bring on.

The next level is self-actualization. This is realizing your personal potential, self-fulfillment, gaining a sense of meaning in life, personal growth and peak experiences. Now you're moving past just getting by, to giving back to society. This is a very, very strong piece in your selling process because you can find ways that will help your prospect know that doing business with you will achieve that for them as well.

Why is psychology important for marketers to understand? People are influenced by many different factors when making purchasing decisions, but before you can select from all the marketing tactics available to you, you need to understand the process your customers go through in making a buying decision. What they're thinking and feeling at each stage will help you determine the best way to reach your potential customers. It's called the "customer journey, " you can spend a lot of time and money on this, but at least start laying a necessary foundation and finding out why customers made individual decisions when they chose to work with you. How can you do that? You survey your customers and prospects. Even surveying people that did not buy from you will provide insight into your product or service. If you notice that someone came to your website and did not buy, and maybe they were on your email list, you can run an automation to send them a quick survey to ask what they did not like about the product or service, or what you could have done differently to earn their business?"

To be able to have insight into your customers' decision-making process is worth its weight in gold!

Considering the steps in the buyers' decision-making process, if we want someone to buy from us, they're going to notice a need in their life. It could be something like hunger. It could be something like a neighbor who had their home broken into, so they don't feel safe.

The next stage once they've realized their need, is they will begin to start researching. Remember in the previous chapter about "zero moment of truth"? When they realize their need, they start searching online. What will they find? At this stage, they realized they have a need, and now they need to get information to meet their need best. You want to be found providing education and helpful resources and get in front of this search process.

Prospects pay attention to information coming from family and friends or other consumers who have used the product or service they are researching; they pay more attention to this than if they saw an advertising message or online ad. They also rely on their feelings about a brand. Maybe they've always grown up with a certain brand and so they trust that because of the brand loyalty passed onto them from their family. It's good to understand the sources that your customers use for their information. It could be personal friends, it could be media, it could be experiential where they've used the product before.

The next stage is the evaluation of alternatives. The prospect begins looking at different brands, and products, and services to select what they perceive is their best choice. Purchases can be divided into two types: "high-involvement and low-involvement." High-involvement usually involves a higher-priced item, and there may be more personal risk involved in making the decision. An example would be buying a house where there are many choices of professionals to work with through the process. An example of a low-involvement purchase would be to buy a pen. You don't need to do much research when you need pens. You go online and buy it, or you go to the store and make the purchase. The evaluation stage is much more drawn-out and complex for high-involvement purchases. For example, people spend lots of time looking at the different models for their next major car purchase, or low-involvement purchases are made with mere brief evaluation of alternatives.

The next stage is making the purchase. The customer takes the information they've gathered in the evaluation stage, and they use it to make the purchase that they decided will help them meet their needs. It's a very simple step, but it's still important to consider because it can be affected by many factors. These factors may include customer service, the ease of the purchase, shipping and return policies, promotions. Many times, people will choose an item just because of free shipping. A customer who's chosen a brand to purchase might change their mind at the last minute if it's too difficult during the buying process. Obviously, entire books have been written on this single stage of the process and closing the sale is crucial to your success.

Combining Authority Selling™ with traditional sales training will certainly take your success to the next level.

Finally, one of the important steps is the post-purchase evaluation. Once the consumer has completed their purchase, they start questioning themselves. Have you ever done research on a product or service after you've bought it? I find myself doing that many times! We want to validate our decision, and this is another perfect stage to integrate social proof.

You must consider these points in your Authority Positioning and Authority Selling™. If you work in an industry where you are providing a higher priced or higher involvement product or service, that decision-making process will require a lot more trust. The consumer will need to see social proof along their journey in researching options and potentially selecting you for their need. Knowing just when to provide these

Authority Positioning Assets at specific points along the buying process is an art form and dedicating yourself to mastering this will pay huge dividends in your business.

There are a lot of key psychological drivers which marketing and sales professionals need to use to choose the most efficient tactic to reach their audience. Let's look at some common ways to use these, and keep in mind, once we have noticed the buying pattern and process our prospects go through, we now need to put a strategy in place to reach out and connect with them.

Reciprocity is one of the most well-known and widely understood psychological drivers in marketing. It says that we feel obligated to give back to someone who's given to us. If we've done a favor for someone, they feel like they owe us; as such, using reciprocity in your sales and marketing is a compelling opportunity. In content marketing, you give away content. Maybe it's a free download or a free trial of your product or your service, and it boosts your sales because customers who receive the free content are more likely to feel compelled to buy from you.

Maybe it's a gift, a large discount, or a free 30-day trial of your software. If you sell a product or service that you can give access to such as software, and you can give prospects thirty days to try it out. While they are using it in their environment, they see how it works, how it would benefit their life; then when the thirty days is up, it is dramatically easier to close the sale because you gave them the free access and they saw results before they purchased.

Another psychological driver is consistency. We like to keep our actions and thoughts consistent; we almost feel compelled to do so. When we act inconsistently, this causes cognitive dissidence, or psychological discomfort in our brain and we must address it. An example is when you find yourself researching that product after you've bought it to confirm your decision, you need to make sure that your thinking is consistent regarding the action of your purchase.

Just like a sales person sticking their foot in the door and physically holding open the doors, they can deliver their pitch; this is where the phrase "foot-in-the-door" comes from! The next psychological driver is where a salesperson asks the customer to make small decisions and then progressively make larger ones. Charitable organizations use this technique when they just ask you to sign a petition and then move on to bigger requests like asking for small amounts of money, and then a larger donation. Another example might be a company conducting a survey that asks participants to like their Facebook page to be a fan of their brand. Then a survey follows up with a sales pitch to point out that since they are a fan of the brand, the next step is to be part of their inner circle and make a purchase.

A foot-in-the-door relies on gaining consent, but the opposite can also be a powerful driver, rejection. This is when a salesperson makes a larger request first, one that's too large. Once the prospect rejects them, they present a smaller request. The person being asked will feel somewhat bad about saying no the first time, and then be more likely to agree to a comparatively reasonable smaller amount. The bigger request, makes the smaller request appear even smaller. Many times the sale is made much more frequently than if you had offered the smaller item first!

In the Authority Selling™ process, you can start off with your highest-priced packages, which sets the frame and gives the buyer the impression that other people are purchasing at that price-point. Many times, your prospect will buy the higher-priced package; but if they don't, you can back down to a smaller package, and it will very likely result in a sale.

The next psychological driver is called loss aversion. We feel the adverse effect of loss so much stronger than the other side of a positive, effective gain, so we try to avoid loss. Think about this. What if you were told by your boss that you were getting a $10 a month raise, or what if you were told by your boss you were losing $10 a month from your paycheck? You would be thinking the $10 raise is minuscule and not very exciting, but on the other hand, if the company cuts your pay by $10, it feels like an outrage! This fear of loss is a necessary driver, so you may be able to weave this into your marketing message to tell the story focusing on taking action now or potentially lose out on specific benefits.

Another psychological driver is scarcity. When supply is limited in quantity or time, we feel a more urgent need to buy. Have you seen more frequent use of countdown timers on both TV and online? An offer expires in two hours and twenty-eight minutes, and they show a countdown timer counting down the seconds…you can just feel your anxiety levels increase if it's an item you are considering buying. That's the principle of scarcity. Increasing urgency and scarcity boosts the value of a product because there's only a limited number. Scarcity is not always ethically because it tends to play on the emotion of fear more than the other psychological principles. For that reason, it can easily be abused. If misused, scarcity can backfire, so it needs to be used sparingly. If you say a deal is going away at a particular time, then you'd better take it down when you said the deadline was set to expire. If someone comes back two or three weeks later and the same deal is there, they realize that you were using false scarcity.

Another psychological driver is called the decoy effect. This leads customers to change their preference between two options when a third, less appealing option is added, so the third option is the decoy. The decoy effect is most commonly seen with price points. For example, a software package may offer two pricing options. One is lower but has fewer features, and the other is much higher with many more features and benefits. If only one of the two is offered, the higher priced item looks really expensive. But if the company added a third higher-priced option and calls it the "executive suite" for example, this will drive sales of the now middle package, because many buyers may think: "I don't need an executive package."

Many times, you will see this in marketing packages displaying three columns. The middle column is a lot larger and may have a banner across it that says "most popular"; they're doing this for a specific purpose because people tend not to want the most expensive, and they tend not to want the least expensive, so they choose the one in the middle!

That leads to another psychological driver which is focusing on fewer options. We often take it for granted that more options naturally will help customers realize that we have more to offer and they will certainly pick one of them. This is not the case because with too many options customers can feel overwhelmed and it can lead them to choose to buy nothing at all because a confused mind never buys. If you have a variety of options you want to present, such as an extensive product line, you need a simpler way to offer your products. You can provide your other choices in a one-time offer at the checkout. If they're online and they're clicking the buy button, you could say, "Before you conclude your sale, would you like to add this to your order?" Maybe on the thank you page after the sale is completed you could say, "Hey, would you like us also to provide this service or this package?" Or even in the email confirmation include a link to a complimentary product other customers buy. Don't forget to include a few testimonials as well! You want to keep things very simple and provide fewer options to keep people from feeling confused or overwhelmed.

Another point to keep in mind is that the buyers are thinking about what the product or service will do for them. Your marketing and sales have to maintain their needs in focus. It's like the old example of everyone's favorite (fictional) radio station, "WiiFM: "What's in it For Me." When you approach Authority Selling™ through the lens of educating and becoming your customers' advocate and helping them make the right decision, keep everything focused on them and their needs, not your products or your unique brand. Make sure that it meets their needs first in an ethical and generous way. How can you over-deliver? This helps build your brand in more ways than just the design of your logo!

Honest, ethical marketers use psychology to influence decision-making based on what customers truly need, not what they think the customers need, or what they want them to buy. Ethical marketers and sales people will use sound techniques. Ethical marketing doesn't make false claims or exaggerate; it backs up what they say with data. Remember, when you are transparent in your marketing and promotions, you'll not only stay on the ethical side, but you will win-over customers who appreciate your honesty. When you are developing your Authority Positioning Portfolio™, make sure that you are positioning yourself as the Expert in that industry as the solution to your prospect's problem, but only in an ethical way. Do not use over-inflated claims that cannot be backed up by research or data.

When you focus on developing your Authority and Expertise and are mentioned in the media, interviewed on a radio show, or have articles published on your blog, make sure you are getting each one of these assets in front of your prospects, strategic alliances, and current customers. This recognition and consistency of repetition are going to help you become the obvious choice when their need for your product or service arises.

Let's talk about repetition in your sales and marketing. People seeing your content frequently is a powerful way to sell your product or service. When you are in the media, and producing your Authority Positioning assets like your interviews or media mentions, repetition works powerfully to set the stage for your Authority Selling™ process. When your target audience sees that you were mentioned here or interviewed there, they may not read every word of that media mention; they may not listen to every word of your interview on a podcast or radio show; but if they see that you're out there frequently many, many, many times, that boosts your Authority Positioning in their eyes. Repetition is crucial.

In today's busy world, there's lots of sales "noise" where brands are vying for your customer's attention. For that reason, people many times will miss your message altogether, or miss an important aspect of it. Repeating your product or your brand name, or even your entire message, helps it to stick in their mind. They may not understand your message the first time they hear it. They may not be ready to hear it. Their situation may have changed since the first time they heard it. Being repetitive and keeping your message out there in front of people is very, very important.

Repeating your message is not as easy as you might imagine. It takes some creativity or else it will just be irritating noise. Repeating the same exact message over and over does not work. You need to make the same core offering and keep the message the same, but you need to use variety by creating text-based marketing materials, videos and visual content, like infographics, and many other media formats. I teach Marketing Strategy at several universities as an adjunct marketing professor, one of the marketing concepts is called IMC which stands for Integrated Marketing Communications. What that means is you're keeping your core message consistent across all of your channels, and you're using a variety of channels as well. If you're only using one marketing channel, it's easy for someone to tune you out. If you only email people, they can quickly click delete or set up a rule in their email provider to not accept your messages or move them directly to the trash folder. I do this, and I'm sure you do as well!

If you only use the phone, people can let it roll to voicemail. You need to have your message where people see it online; they see something in their mailbox; they're getting a voicemail message from you; they see it in their email inbox. You get the picture!

Here's a tip: Let's say that you have a database of your customers, prospects, and strategic alliances and you have their cell phone numbers because these days so many people use their mobile number as their primary number anyway. What if you send a quick voicemail or an email out to your list say, "Hey, I am so honored to be interviewed on this podcast. Here's the link if you would like to listen to it." What if you also posted that on your social media? Those are the obvious ones, along with putting it on your website.

You must use a variety of marketing channels to get the word out every single time you have an Authority Positioning asset created. This is applying repetition and consistency correctly. But is there a potential for too much repetition? There could be, so you want to make sure that you're not sending out too many things; too often. If you were interviewed on four radio shows this week, spread it out. Send out one a month for the next four months. Don't only use one channel, test what happens to your sales or your traffic or your response when you distribute your content on one channel compared to another. Make sure that you do more of the things that your prospects and your target audience are responding to. That is an important activity to ensure that you are doing.

These easy strategies will help your target audience realize that you are an Authority and that your expertise is very applicable to them because it is solving a problem that they have. How did you discover that problem? You did some research. You listened to their feedback on surveys sent after they purchased. The more engaged your customers and prospects are in your brand, the easier it is to provide what they need and increase your revenue without being a pushy salesperson.

AUTHORITY SELLING™ EXECUTION TIP:

As you develop your Authority Portfolio Assets, make sure that the person in your firm who updates marketing collateral has easy access to them in one convenient location. This place needs to be conducive to adding new assets as you build them. Each new media mention, interview, customer testimonial or book you publish needs to be added to this file and posted on your website. This could be a shared folder on your network drive or a Google Doc etc. You need to be able to use these Authority assets in your marketing and promotions without having to hunt all over for them.

AUTHORITY SELLING™ ACTION GUIDE:

Think about your own decision-making process for finding a new dentist for yourself. What are you thinking, feeling, and asking yourself at each step of the process?

_____

_____

_____

_____

_____

_____

_____

_____

_____

_____

What information do you need at each step?

Now think about the decision making process your customers go through when deciding whether to buy your products or services.
See if you can answer the same questions.

_____

_____

_____

_____

_____

_____

_____

_____

_____

_____

_____

Authority Selling™ Strategy:
Persuasive Selling

The art of persuasive selling for people who hate to sell

When using Authority Selling™ and the Authority Positioning Portfolio™ you will be building, consider how it will be perceived by your audience. We touched earlier on not being cocky or prideful. When you think about selling, does something inside of you just make you feel very uncomfortable like you are bothering your prospect? You've probably seen all of the recommendations from other sales experts that say you need to have long sales copy to convince your prospects that your service or your product is the obvious choice. While this can be effective, think about how YOU respond to long text. Do you have time to read through super-long sales pages, even if it's a product or service you are interested in? You obviously need to make sure you include enough content and data to help your prospect make a buying decision, but I have seen copy that repeated the stacked offer 3-4 times pushing the page-count to 30+ pages!

Have you been approached by a vendor in the mall who wants to try to sell you their product or when you walk into a store, the sales clerk comes up to you asking you how they can help? It doesn't have to be this way in your business when you use Authority Selling™. In fact, you'll be far more successful in the long run, and make more sales, if you take an entirely different approach and infuse your Authority and your Expert positioning in a caring and educational way.

If you hate the idea of selling, then you're going to love this chapter.

The internet has changed the world of marketing and sales. Marketers can no longer use the same exact techniques online that worked even just a few years ago. The attitude and behavior pattern of your prospects has changed and to be successful, you must change with them. How do you know that the patterns and buying habits have changed? Because prospects and customers go online to do research before even contacting you... and many times before even arriving at your website.

You must be an educator and advocate for your clients and your prospects, and you must be seen as an Authority who cares about the needs of your target audience. How can you do this? Again, by giving them information to help make their decision about your product or service. If you have created your Authority Positioning assets correctly, your prospects will easily find your educational content. Make sure that the title includes the problem your target audience has and your solution so that when they are out looking for these solutions online, the assets will come up in their search results.

The key to building relationships is to focus on your customer's needs. You must listen to them and understand their problems and desires. Only then can you offer your products and services to them with the best chance of a positive buying decision. You'll waste your time trying to convince them to buy products that they never wanted in the first place. Customers are looking online for information already, and you can be there to fill their need. Build your Expertise by providing answers to their questions…before they even ask!

Prospective customers visit your website because they feel you're offering what they need. How do they know that? Because they've seen in their research that you may have the answer to their problem. How did they find that? They went looking online for information to solve a problem they have.

If you've done this the right way, journalists will do the same thing when they're writing a story; they will search for content and Experts they can quote in their news story. You need to be there online with solutions to problems so that prospects as well as journalists find your content and potentially reach out to you.

How would it look if your prospect Googles a particular problem that they're having and they see links where you've been featured solving that very problem? Maybe you were interviewed on a radio show. Perhaps you've been in the media. Maybe you wrote a book. All of these things are incredible assets. When you can build this out the right way, you have a robust Authority Selling™ platform that pre-frames you in such a powerful way! Much of the selling begins before they even contact you and the frustrating thing is many times you will not even know that you did not get the phone call or the Internet request.

Why is this? Because they've gone to a competitor that already is positioning themselves as the Authority and the Expert in your industry!

Offer what prospects need and invite them to join a dialogue with you. A quick phone call. A quick live chat on your website, sometimes people want an answer to their question a lot faster than sending an email, opening a support ticket. There are many companies who offer a live chat service for your website. Just Google "live chat" and you will see plenty of choices from $15-$40 a month. Pick one that fits your budget, because this is a wonderful way to be approachable to your target audience and help prospects and customers really feel connected to you and your brand.

So what is an Expert anyway? It's someone who knows more than the client does about a particular topic. You may feel like you are not an Expert in your field but think about your last customer or client that you brought on board with your company or the last sale that you made. Did they ask you a few questions? Did you answer their questions? When you confidently answer their questions, you are an Expert in their eyes! Keep this in mind because it will help you realize that based your industry knowledge, you ARE an Expert!

Expert status may be credentials and visibility, but it also is quality content and confident response to questions that your prospects have.

Expertise is a critical element in marketing, in particular on the internet because online customers are looking for answers and they want it from trusted sources who clearly know what they're talking about. If you can establish yourself as an Expert on your specific topics, your products and service will virtually sell themselves because they come to you pre-sold. Having a blog is an excellent and simple place to start, plus Google likes to see fresh content. Having a blog allows you the platform to begin writing about your Expertise.

Depending on how you like to produce your content, another area people can find your information would be to start a YouTube channel. Make sure that you have a YouTube channel set up with your business name and record short video snippets of these practical solutions to the problem your target audience has faced. It doesn't have to be long. It doesn't have to be professional. It could be you holding up your phone and walking in the park and giving a quick talk. Very easily, in a short, 2-minute video you can have assets out there which get found online quickly.

The "Expertise Gap" is the difference between what you know about a particular topic and what your audience knows. In other words, it's what you already know how to do, but others haven't learned yet. That lends itself to you being seen as an Expert. Understanding this is an important part of building your expertise. You have to understand your customers and their level of knowledge about your topic. For instance, if you have lived overseas for thirty years, you're an Expert. If this was your industry focus, write your content for people who are just setting off trying to move overseas as you were years ago. Maybe you have a level of expertise in finding the best bed and breakfast in foreign countries. That lends itself to building your Authority Selling™ so that when you are looking to sell that product or service you have, they are predisposed to buying from you because they see you as that Expert. Your bio should say more than just,

"I'm an avid skier." It needs to show your Expert knowledge and experience.

A good way to do this is building that portfolio we have been learning about. Publish articles wherever you can. Create books to sell on Kindle. Write a guest post for other blogs. Join your industry organizations. Participate in their events. Conduct seminars locally for local groups. See if you can teach a class at a local community college. That is an excellent Authority Positioning asset when you include that in your bio and your Authority Positioning Portfolio™. You can reach out to a prospect before your upcoming meeting and say, "Hey, here are some things to take a look at before we connect for our meeting next week. This is an interview I did recently and a flyer for the class that I taught at our local community college on the same topic we're going to be talking about."

When you walk in the door or get on the phone with them, they are already pre-framed and conditioned to view you as the Expert because you are! Make sure to add an "About Me" or "Press" page on your website and list all of these assets where every time you get a new opportunity, you add it on this page.

It's impossible to establish your expertise overnight. It takes time and dedicated effort. You have to learn about your topic, read lots of content and build your credentials. However, each year that you're out there adds tremendously to your reputation as an Expert. Just make sure that you're compiling each and every one of these Authority Positioning assets so that people can see how many solutions that you're providing.

To really understand your customers, you need hard data that they can rely on. You have to listen to your customers' feedback as well as the conversations they have online. You can learn about people's thoughts and feelings through comments on blogs and from social media. You can also ask people individually. There are a lot of tools that can help you know what your target audiences' problem areas are. If you were to set up Hoot Suite or Tweet Deck or Sprout Social or whatever social media tool that you would like to use; put in certain keywords so that when those keywords are mentioned in social media, you can see what people are saying…and respond pointing them to your educational content.

Now you begin hearing all of the issues and frustrations that your audience is facing. This becomes a huge help as you are structuring your Authority Positioning Portfolio™ assets. The next interview that you do with a podcaster you can ask to have it titled including the solution to the problem you have heard about. Listening is super important.

Remember that people don't like to be sold, but they like to buy. How can they make that buying decision? They need to realize that you are the obvious choice. Even if you are well-positioned as an Authority, if your product or service does not meet their needs, they still won't choose you; no matter how many interviews or books you've written, because you have to make sure all of these come together in the right formula. Some people are more receptive to certain types of media than others. If you handed someone a copy of your book, that may be wonderful but maybe they would rather hear the two or three recent interviews you did on that same topic.

Here's another tip on what to create, and how to build it. Think of the Top 10 "Frequently Asked" questions you get about your product or service. If right now you listed the Top 10 "Frequently Asked" questions that you get about your product or service, could you quickly write down ten? I would think you could. Then move right into the Top 10 "Should-Ask" questions. These are the questions that people don't even know to ask but if they did ask them they would get a much deeper understanding of your product or service. Once you list your Top 10 "Frequently Asked" questions, you could then take it to the next level and list ten "Should-Ask" questions because you know your product or service and you know the questions that people should be asking that would further separate you from your competitor. These twenty "Frequently Asked" questions and "Should-Ask" questions then become the basis for your Authority Positioning assets.

How could you use these? Maybe you make a focused effort to get interviewed on a podcast, and you want to cover "Frequently Asked" question number one, two and three. Then maybe the next time you're interviewed you want to include the "Should-Ask" questions one, two and three. You make sure that the content is covered so that when you use these interviews, and the media mentions you, the title of the interview answers the questions that your prospects have in their mind as they search online researching solutions.

There's no such thing as too much information as it relates to educational content. Remember, if you can educate in an overabundance of ways, on a variety of platforms, it reinforces your teaching. The key is to present enough information to your prospect that it answers the questions that are going on in their mind. When you can cover those "Should-Ask" questions, they're almost thinking, "Aha, that's a great question." Then when you answer it, you're reducing many of the objections that they may have when you do connect with them. Create that wide variety of content to show your audience what your product or service can do for them. Educate them to shortens your sales cycle.

Content should be written in a conversational style that's not stiff or too formal. A lot of sales copy sounds very corporate, or it seems like people are making too big of a deal out of that one point. People can sense that. Your copy needs to be written as though it's someone telling a good friend or family member about the product or service.

One way is to keep your writing style on target is to record yourself reading it and listen to the recording. That will help the way that you are presenting your content. Remember, if it's too much like a textbook or corporate-style content, people will not relate or respond to it in the way you would like them to. The more conversational and open your style is, the easier it is to make your point that your product or service is the solution to their problem.

Another tip is to make your content easy to scan. The reader should be able to skim through the text and understand your main points. Break it up into bullet points, smaller paragraphs, shorter sentences, give sections a headline that summarizes what it's about. If you're writing that blog post or even your book on Kindle or a paperback on Amazon, make sure it's easy to scan because people are busy and they may not read every word. If they can scan that page and see that that content is exciting to them, then they will read it deeper, but even if all they did was skim your content, you want them to get the most important points.

You need to focus your sales content on the pain or frustration that your products solve for the reader…don't be afraid to go deep on this because you really want to have them feel their discontent! Now think about this from the Authority Selling™ perspective. Include examples of how you were interviewed on a podcast talking about this very problem. Maybe you say, "This is why I wrote my latest book published on Amazon." This is an excellent way to integrate your Authority Positioning assets.

AUTHORITY SELLING™ ACTION GUIDE:

Make a list of your 10 "Frequently Asked" questions you get asked.

_____

_____

_____

_____

_____

_____

_____

_____

_____

_____

_____

_____

_____

_____

_____

_____

_____

Make a list of the 10 "Should-Ask" questions
your prospects should be asking.

_____

_____

_____

_____

_____

_____

_____

_____

_____

_____

_____

_____

_____

_____

_____

_____

_____

_____

Think about what you know that others don't, even if it's very basic. Note at least the three areas where people could benefit from your knowledge.

_____

_____

_____

_____

_____

_____

_____

_____

_____

_____

_____

_____

_____

_____

_____

_____

Brainstorm at least 5 ways or places where you
can demonstrate your knowledge.

_____

_____

_____

_____

_____

_____

_____

_____

_____

_____

_____

_____

_____

_____

_____

_____

_____

Authority Selling™ Strategy:

Social Proof: Using the power of social influence to increase your sales.

Social proof is so important because it allows your prospects to rely on the past positive experiences others have had with you and your company, even if they don't know the person that provided the social proof. In short, social proof is a review or a testimonial.

Think about how many times you have looked online for a restaurant, and looked at the reviews, and moved on to the next restaurant because the reviews that you saw were negative. Social proof is one of the many strategies and techniques that marketers rely on to convince you that their product is worth your hard-earned cash because it taps into the fundamental human characteristic, the need to be like others! In our desire to conform, we often give in and buy whatever marketers have to offer.

But, think about it from the perspective of the marketer. If we realize that our prospects want to be like others and they respond to positive social proof, how can we use social proof in our business without being sneaky or deceptive?

Social proof is really just a modern name given to something that has existed since humans formed their first communities. What's at work with social proof is more than just the desire to conform, or a marketers' attempt to persuade. It's part of everything we do. Imagine you're trying to decide between two restaurants for dinner. One is nearly empty, but the other one has a line stretching around the corner.

Assuming you're not in a hurry, which restaurant do you choose? And, now let's interject ethics into that example. Obviously, if time were not an issue, you would choose the one with the line stretching around the corner or a full parking lot because that means that they are popular and the people are probably coming back after being there the first time. The ethics come into play when, if you were the manager of that restaurant, and you paid people to stand in line, and you paid people to park their cars in your lot to give the impression that your restaurant is fantastic. It happens. That is a breach of ethics because it's not a valid representation of your restaurant.

It's a part of everyone's life. It's a keystone of any marketing strategy, and it's a technique that you need to be incorporating into your marketing plan. It also is a powerful Authority Positioning technique because of how it influences the decision people are making when they see your client's and customer's testimonials and reviews. They would trust them, even if they didn't know the person who left the review. You are the obvious choice because you've given excellent service and that elevates you to an Expert Authority status in that industry because you have earned that social proof.

AUTHORITY SELLING™ EXECUTION TIP:

Along with your Authority Positioning assets, include testimonials as social proof. What better way to close a sale easier than to show your prospect that you were recently quoted in a media outlet, interviewed on a radio show, wrote a book and also have a handful of testimonials from raving fan clients!

Social proof is a psychological phenomenon where people base their decision, or course of action, based on what's going on around them. It's most powerful in situations where you're not sure what the right course of action is or if you're not confident about your decision.

Think of this; negative social proof is very powerful. If you were looking at restaurants for dinner, and there were ten positive reviews and two negative reviews we'll you might feel like that's fine because the positive outweigh the negative; that's a pretty good percentage. But, people's attention focuses on that negative review. You want to do as much as you can to keep your social proof positive or at least build so many positive reviews that they bury the few negative!

It works on all levels of society. It's present in any advertisement where you see messages like 8,356 people downloaded this software program this week. Or, this product is recommended by nine out of ten doctors. Have you ever been booking travel and you see the counter on the hotel or airline page you're looking at showing that 56 people are viewing this reservation currently? That is an element of scarcity infused with social proof which are very powerful drivers that we can use in our marketing. I heard a speaker at a seminar who said he does not ever go to a new movie or read a new book unless he's had at least two or three of his friends come to him raving about it. What groups of people or situations have influence on you?

When you are thinking about Authority Selling™, and you are building your Authority Positioning Portfolio™, make sure to use reviews and testimonials from happy customers and clients. You want your network to know when you were interviewed on the radio or podcast or to learn that you wrote your book, you also want them to know every single time someone gives you a good review. Every single time! You may feel like it's enough just to include them on the testimonials page on your website.

But think about it, most people don't go searching through your site every few weeks to see if you have new testimonials. But if they're on their Facebook, and they see your logo, and your brand name and phone number, and your picture that says "Another five star review from Betty L," and it gives her review of your product or service, and it's in their Facebook stream because they like you on Facebook; that's a powerful way to project your positive social proof and build your Authority Positioning. Especially when they click that they like the photo and then their friends see it and can read about your excellent service!

Social proof in the form or reviews or testimonials or statistics on customer satisfaction tells the prospective customer that this is a company they can trust. If your testimonials page has dozens, and dozens, and dozens of reviews, at some point, you may think it's enough and that you don't need to collect them anymore. But I would recommend that you need to collect them to the end of time! Even if you have 200, or 400, or 900 reviews, people will start scrolling down through those testimonials and realize: "This company is trustworthy because they are cranking such excellent service that people are raving about their product or service."

Having consistency, frequency, and repetition also applies to the social proof you're building. This ties in the power of the psychological drivers in marketing that we covered earlier!

Social proof is also an important factor in driving people to make a purchase or sign up for something on a website. If you're marketing a product or service and you wanted to put out a whitepaper or video series or a case study, you have to sell the opt-in.

Think about those boxes that say "Download this report," and it asks for an email address; people realize that they're going to get follow-up e-mails. You have to sell the fact that they will benefit from that download so having some social proof on the download page is another powerful way for you to increase your Authority. Include testimonials on your download page expressing how valuable the information in the report was to that person so that it increases the download success rate.

This sells the current step in your sales process so the prospect can get to the next level which allows you to communicate more with them.

When someone has bought your product or service and has given you a review, you should e-mail that out, or push it out to your social media channels; but could you also put that on your order page?

Like we were saying earlier about downloading the report; if you have an order page to purchase your product or service and the buy button that they click to put in their credit card information has two or three reviews and testimonials, you increase the success rate of your cart.

This is another powerful way to increase your Authority Selling™ because that social proof is helping to "sell the click," to "sell the download," to "sell the purchase." They may have read your report, read your website, listened to your interview, scanned your book, looked at the media that you're mentioned in, but still when they get to that order page and are ready to put their credit card number in; there still may be hesitation. If at that last stage you can use social proof of customers like themselves who have purchased that product or service and given rave reviews, that helps to sell that final step in the process to bring on a new customer.

One of the most common sources of social proof is your past clients who have purchased and used your product. When you get feedback from your past customers or clients, and they are explaining what they like about your product or service, there are a few benefits you must realize.

1.   It reinforces your product or service benefits to the customer. In a subtle way, the act of writing the review makes them remember their experience with your brand and how they liked working with and the benefit your product gave them.

2.   It is excellent research to be able to see what it was that attracted them to your product or service.

3.   It is fantastic social proof to use in your marketing because it engenders trust.

4. It reinforces to you and your team the value that you bring to your customers and clients. When you feel confident that you are adding huge value to your products and services, it is easier to sell.

The next step is to identify how you're going to get your social proof. Gathering social proof is an ongoing process, and it has to be part of your marketing operations, but you need a plan for doing it consistently. Don't think that doing it just once is a good idea. Just like we have said in this book, being interviewed one time is not enough. You must have a way that will allow you to collect reviews and testimonials quickly and consistently.

Put yourself in the shoes of your potential customer for a moment. What kind of information would remove all doubt from their minds and help them make a purchasing decision to choose you? What would they be looking for regarding social proof as they're shopping for solutions online and offline? Start by figuring out what is relevant and meaningful to your current clients and then use it in your messaging to prospects. Take into account where prospects are in your sales process.

The type of social proof you use might change at different points of the sales funnel. At each stage of the funnel, keep in mind what action you want the consumer to take and what they already know or feel about your company. Maybe at the point of downloading your initial report, to sell that click, you may need to have an interview that you've done and a testimonial from a past customer or client talking about what they're going to download. For example, "This video series was so helpful, I took these lessons away from it and was able to put things to work in my business right away." Being able to have different social proof touchpoints is very powerful.

Position your social proof so that it clearly states how you successfully solve the reader's problem. You could also address the problems your customers are anticipating. This gets back to the Top 10 "Frequently Asked" questions and Top 10 "Should-Ask" questions.

If these are correctly formatted and properly answered, and used throughout your sales and marketing process as assets, now your prospects come through your sales funnel learning so much more than they would have if your competitors sent them a brochure or a flyer. They come to speak with you fully educated and ready to make a buying decision.

Another key point is to have your customer focus on their decision-making process and the positive result they experienced. For example: "I did not initially think this product would work for me because my unique problem is ____, but what I discovered was _____." This is so powerful because other people have the same struggle and concern in their mind. They may have doubted the legitimacy or the claims of products or services like yours; but when they see that someone else questioned it as well before they purchased, they really relate to that testimonial, that social proof at a much deeper level.

If possible, include a picture of the customer because it makes a more engaging social proof. Keep in mind, when setting up your process for collecting and using reviews and testimonials, it has to be simple and easy. You can have a lot of bells and whistles, and pictures, and things like that, but the best testimonial …is a testimonial that is done.

There is an automated review software platform that I provide my clients that allows them to set up an automated series of requests for their customers to complete their feedback. When it is a positive response, the review filter will ask them also to put it online on Google, or Yelp, or one of many review sites. If it is a negative response, it will ask them to go deeper and provide more detail and submit it; but it does not encourage them to continue online, the completed form is sent to the manager or owner. It also automatically creates a custom branded graphic with their logo and phone number and the content of the review the customer left and automatically distributes it to their website and all of their social media channels.

Using a solution like this helps consistently get new reviews to use in your marketing and build your online reputation without having to remember to follow up and ask. It's an automated solution that takes about 15 minutes per month making your request for testimonials automated, consistent, and easy.

You can also get testimonials from third-party sites like local business directories. Remember, people will go to the local directories like Yelp, Super Pages, and Better Business Bureau and they will put reviews there as well. You want to monitor the directory sites to make sure if, and when, someone ever puts a review on those sites that you are immediately notified so you can respond. Having a software do this for you is imperative because you will not check every single day on dozens of those sites to see if there's a new review. You need to have something that will notify you automatically.

Inevitably you will get bad feedback once in a while, and you want to make sure if there is a negative review, you learn from it and that you change things in your procedures to ensure the issue doesn't come up again.

Testimonials aren't the only tactic for social proof; case studies are a customer's stories that are longer and more involved than a simple testimonial. Case studies highlight positive experiences your customers have had with your product, and since they're longer, they allow you to provide more detail. Typically, a case study is a story that tells how a person used your product or service and it demonstrates how others can use the product or service as well. The best case studies are very visual, so use images of the customer, your product, or graphs with data supporting a particular point of research you want to show.

It's much better to say, "I gained 2,325 more e-mail subscribers," or "She increased her sales by 43.5%," than something like, "My e-mail subscribers grew." Having specific facts will help you successfully make key points in your case study which answer the questions that are in the reader's mind.

- What were things like for them before they purchased and used your product and service?

- How is their life different now and what specific results have they gained?

Paint a picture that describes the before and after. Think about all of the weight loss ads you see, try to show the reader visually the result they can achieve.

Also, like any good story, make your main character the subject of the testimonial, as relatable as possible.

Do you see what we're doing here? We're using social proof & "story-selling" to communicate powerful results. I want you to make sure that you pick up on this point. In a case study, you're using specific facts focused on how you're solving a problem to your target audience's issues. The case study is social proof. You're using "story-selling" to bring it to life, and these are powerful communication tools.

Statistics also offer a great source of social proof because they display credibility and trust. Some messages that tell the reader that 50 people have purchased this product this week is a helpful way to encourage purchases, but remember, don't fake your statistics. Make sure that they are actual statistics and real numbers because trust and transparency are so important. Whenever your company or website is mentioned in any media outlet, that's a great opportunity for social proof. These types of remarks are particularly impressive. Rather than evidence from regular people and customers, this is an acknowledgment that comes from a trusted 3rd-party source. Display these high profile mentions wherever possible on your website, social media profile, and any other channels of communication.

Create a press release section on your site and keep it updated on the latest news and PR information about your company. It shows that you're active in the media. Show off any good press that you get. If possible, show an image or a video of your clients or customers. When you put a human face on your social proof, it's even more powerful.

Include your client testimonials in your weekly blog or e-mail newsletter. Tweet the results of a new survey or statistic that have been provided by a user. Work social proof into your webinars and podcasts. These are very powerful ways to keep that building for your portfolio. You always need to collect, manage, and publish social proof on an ongoing basis to build your Authority Positioning Portfolio™. This goes a long way in your Authority Selling™

AUTHORITY SELLING™ ACTION GUIDE:

List clients who could help build social proof?

_____

_____

_____

_____

_____

_____

_____

_____

_____

_____

_____

_____

_____

_____

_____

_____

_____

Select at least three ways for your own business to attract and maintain a steady stream of testimonials from your customers. Note where in your sales process you could insert testimonials.

_____

_____

_____

_____

_____

_____

_____

_____

_____

_____

_____

_____

_____

_____

_____

Authority Selling™ Strategy:

Interviewing Influencers
Building your Authority by Interviewing Experts

When you begin interviewing Influencers in your industry, you will be able to expand your reputation and boost your business by aligning yourself with leaders that your target audience knows, likes and trusts. Influencers are well-known Experts in your field, and they offer a wonderful way to attract new customers and clients to yourself and expand the reputation of your business. This takes Authority Selling™ to a new level which will elevate your brand far beyond your competitors.

Connecting with known Influencers and interviewing them will build your credibility as an Expert in your own right and show you to be a valuable resource for your market. Some of the most popular books in history are based on this exact concept. "Think and Grow Rich" was a compilation of interviews with well-known Influencers of their day.

Research your industry and look at some of the past or upcoming conferences to make a list of the keynote speakers. If the conference organizer has thought enough to pay this keynote speaker to speak at their event, this is an industry Influencer that you should get to know. Just contact them and ask if they would be open to doing a 20-minute phone interview with you on the topic they spoke about at the recent event.

Once the interview is completed, begin getting that content out on your social media, your blog and consider setting up a podcast channel. This is a very easy and inexpensive process, and you can find tutorials online that will walk you through each step.

Your interview content aligns your brand with the Influencer, and when people in your Circle of Influence see that you interviewed them, they not only learn tips from the interview, but you begin to be seen on a higher level yourself.

As part of your Influencer marketing, the goal is to reach out to someone who is well-known as an Expert in the field. The result is valuable content for your audience and exposure to more potential clients. New people who are searching for the Influencer online will find your interview, and they'll likely start following you as well.

AUTHORITY SELLING™ EXECUTION TIP:

For a small amount of money, you can have your interviews transcribed using Rev.com, Fiverr.com or have a family member do it. Add the text content of your interview on your blog in addition to the audio format. This is important because Google likes to see fresh content that's related to your area of expertise.

Before you feel like this is too much work, just take it a step at a time and start off with a basic and simple process; don't spend a lot of money on equipment. Set up a Free Conference Call HD account and just record the interview. Then you can pay a small amount to get a professional intro added before the interview so that it sounds professional. Then simply post the audio on your blog with a summary of the interview and the guest's bio and then send your blog link through your social media channels and your next email newsletter. Even if this is all you do to start off, you will be making great strides in establishing your Authority Positioning.

Remember that recording interviews with industry leaders, even if they are not well-known, builds your credibility, positions yourself as an Authority in your niche and you create extremely valuable content that helps your audience solve problems and informs them of current trends in the market. You become a resource of education and knowledge for them.

Think about what we've been talking about throughout this book so far about determining the pain points that your target audience experiences and the solutions you provide to solve their problems. You created your Top 10 "Frequently Asked" questions and "Should-Ask" questions. Now you can begin to bring on Experts to your interview series who can speak about these topics, discussing them from an educational standpoint.

Your audience is very interested because it speaks to an issue they are currently facing and as they're searching online for solutions to that problem, they have a good chance to find your interview because you included specific keywords and the Expert's name in your blog post title. The chance that they reach out to you for more information has increased. If you had not researched the issues and brought on a guest to interview about it, they may have never found you.

Another benefit of interviewing Experts is that they typically have a large following. When you send them the link to their interview once it is published, ask if they can send it out to their social media audience to help bring awareness to the issues discussed on the show. Now their followers see you in the same light as they see the Expert that they already respect; this can get you extra exposure from their audience!

Interviewing Influencers and Authorities is such a useful technique that some businesses are entirely built around the approach. I follow people who do this as a full-time business model. Experts like John Lee Dumas and Andrew Warner interview Influencers and authorities every single day on their podcasts…many times seven days a week!

Maybe you're not going to schedule your interviews every day and maybe that's not going to be the sole focus of your business, but this can be a fantastic business development plan to open up doors to close more business for you because it's positioning yourself as an Authority.

Consider taking this approach to the next level; what would happen if you interviewed a series of Experts on a topic in your industry? What if you then asked their permission to compile that into a multi-author book? Now you become someone who is putting together a book that your target audience can download and read interviews from these influencers, and your brand is the one that put it together!

The first step is to identify some industry Authorities and Experts who can help you gain exposure and increase your visibility. You need to choose the right people who not only have a huge following but will help you achieve your specific business goals, while at the same time that they're known and respected by your target audience.

In many sales books, we are taught that the person who controls the conversation with questions is the one who is viewed as the one in control. That's why we should listen more than we speak and use question-based selling strategies.

Think of interviewing Authorities, Experts and Influencers in your industry in the exact same way. You're asking questions. You're aligning with this respected Authority. The people listening are your target audience, prospects, strategic alliances who hear you guiding that conversation with well thought-out questions and this elevates your Authority dramatically.

When you are looking for industry Authorities and Influencers to interview, make sure that they are relevant to your business. It should be someone who's in your same industry, or would be a resource to your industry; otherwise the new followers that they attract won't do much good for you. Obviously, you should try to choose people to interview that have lots of reach. It's not the only criteria because sometimes you don't know that.

You have to do a little bit of research and look at their social media following on Twitter, Facebook, and LinkedIn. Their social media reach should not be the only focus, but it is a bonus when you do find an Authority and an Influencer who has a large fan base.

Consider looking at "Klout," which is the online tool highlighting people that are already being listened to because of their influence. Klout is a paid service that gives a score for everyone that's highly visible online. You can prioritize and rank the quality of your Influencers based on that. You can go through some of the scores and look for people in your industry. This is a great indicator of people to approach for your interviews. You can learn valuable information about who they are and who their influencers are.

On LinkedIn, there's a place down at the bottom of the profile that shows their "Influencers." You can pick up a whole lot of information that way and tell whether they would be relevant to your business or not and look for a way to connect with them.

Amazon is a great resource for researching. Look through books in your industry and find people that have a new book coming out. You don't need even to look for authors who are highly ranked because when you look for authors who have a new book out, you can be sure they are looking to get attention for their book. They've written a book, and they may love to come on your podcast.

Beyond web and social, there are good ways to find Influencers offline. Look at industry publications. Maybe even you can find an online publication in your industry or a magazine you can subscribe to. Subscribe to a magazine for $20 or look for the digital version of their publication. Look at who some of the contributors are. Who wrote some articles? Who are the Experts speaking at events that the publication is putting on? This is an excellent way to build your list of potential interview guests. Look up podcasts in your industry; consider podcast hosts. Consider the guests that they have. Some podcasts have guests or interviews in every episode that can be a goldmine of wonderful ideas. Look at video channels like Vimeo and YouTube.

At first, you need to create a larger list of potential Authorities and Influencers that you can interview because you need to narrow it down. Start with a list of 50 and put it on a spreadsheet. List their names, their websites, Klout score or followers that they have as well as their area of expertise.

At this point, you need to begin your engagement plan. You need to start thinking about how you're going to interact with these Influencers, but do it in an appropriate way where you are not approaching them and right off the bat and asking for an interview. The right way to do this is to start interacting with them in a casual way; start following them on social media and respond to a post that they made on Facebook or LinkedIn. Leave comments that are relevant and interesting and try to contribute some value, but be genuine about it.

Think about this: when you get notifications from LinkedIn, they come right to you. LinkedIn is a very personal, direct social media platform. When you are putting comments on LinkedIn posts, the Influencer themselves typically will get the comment. It's pretty rare that they have an administrative assistant monitor their LinkedIn account.

Decide how you can create value for them. If they have a product or book that you can buy and then contact them and say: "I just bought your book and chapter six was so wonderful because_____." Let them know some points that you appreciated about their book. Promote their book for them in your social media and tag them. This is going to capture their attention.

Then, of course, you need to approach them. Send them an email. There are many tools that can help you find someone's email address. There's one called Email Hunter, which will give you some probable suggestions for an email address for the Expert you are trying to connect with and I have found that it's very reliable.

If you've interacted on social media, you can send them a direct message. Once you've gotten some attention, in a good way, with that Authority and Influencer, ask them a question. "I've got an interview show called _____, and I'd love to interview you. Would you be free for a twenty-minute phone interview in the next few weeks?" It's a simple question and if you've done it the right way, many times you're going to get an affirmative answer.

Now it's time to start thinking about how to conduct a productive interview that meets your marketing objectives and one that will help to promote the Influencer as well as your brand. You want to decide on the business topic that will be the focus of your interview with them. Many times you're going to look on their website and see some of the things that they're working on, or a book they have just written.

You want to send them confirmation of essential details like the call-in number and the password for the conference line. Be very clear on the time and date and especially make sure you remember to convert the time zones. You would hate to have your guest on the line, and you're calling in at a different time! Not good. Many times this is handled by a scheduling tool like Time Trade or Schedule Once. You can easily send them the link so they can then see what some upcoming slots that you have available that fit their schedule. Then when they put in their contact details and the time, the scheduling service, will send them and yourself the confirmation and then a reminder as well. These services, many times will also do the automatic conversion for time zones as well save you from an embarrassing moment!

Before your interview, make sure you have their bio and a high-resolution headshot. Right before you start recording, you might want to make sure you're introducing them correctly. Ask if they prefer to be called "founder of" their company or "President of." They'll appreciate that. If their name is hard to pronounce, ask the best way to pronounce their name.

Focus on them as the interview guest. If they have a non-profit, they're working with that's close to their heart; this would be a fantastic point to include in your interview. You should always have a list of good questions before the beginning of the interview making sure they're open-ended questions which allow the guest to talk at length.

Here are some questions that you can use to customize for your interview:

- Where and how do you do your best work?

- Who has had the biggest influence on you?

- What was the most pivotal moment for you in your business?

- What's your biggest challenge?

- What challenges do you see people face today?

- What has surprised you most along your journey in business?

- How do you structure your daily or weekly schedule?

- How do you balance work and life?

- What advice would you give to our audience?

These questions will help you get the interview off the ground easily. Again, you may have a list of 10 questions before you start your interview, but may only cover 3 of them because you've gone so deep... and that's perfectly fine! Here's something that you want to keep in mind too. When you have your list of questions, you want to begin crossing them off as you go so you don't accidentally ask them again. It sounds like an obvious point but if you have 5-10 questions and ask question number one, draw a line through it or if it's on your computer, just delete it on your notepad. Now you know how many questions you have left to keep going. That's a vital part.

Keep an eye on the clock. If you said it's going to be twenty minutes, make sure that you're starting to wrap up the interview at about 17 or 18 minutes so that you can ask them if they have any final thoughts. Then give them a chance to provide the best way that people can get to know them better and learn more about their business. An important point to keep in mind is treating them as an Expert. You're respecting their time, and you're going to set that time limit and stick to it. If you find yourself running out of time, just start dropping some of the questions at the end. Keeping in mind that that interview guest is doing you a favor, so if you start seeing that you're about halfway through the time you've allotted and you're two questions in, maybe just pick one more substantive question to go deeper on and leave it at that.

One time I interviewed a very well-known Influencer in my industry and at the beginning of the interview, he said I have 17 minutes…we were done in 16 minutes because I watched the clock to make sure we were done on-time. You need to be very cautious of their time. Some Influencers take time out of their busy schedule for an interview with someone that they don't even know because they're just genuinely nice people. Give them an idea of what to expect after the interview. Tell them when you're done, after you've stopped the recording, you can chat for a minute or two. This is when you thank them for their time and let them know where it's going to be published and tell them that you'll send them a link so that they can use it in their business promotions. Tell them you would appreciate it if they would post it out through their social media channels.

Now it is time to promote your interview and boost your Authority Positioning! Make it very, very simple so that when you're done with each interview, it's a simple process to promote it on your blog and your social media.

A good way to extend your reach is to identify groups or other professional forums online or on social media that you can post your interview. You can simply say something like: "I was so privileged to have interviewed _____, here's the link to the show where we cover topics including_____. Let me know what you think!"

Simple! When the members of the group listen to your interview, they're viewing you as an Authority right along with the Expert you're interviewing. Are you seeing the power of positioning yourself and amplifying each one of the assets in your Authority Positioning Portfolio™?

Make a goal of doing one interview a month and then whatever frequency that you can handle, I would say to you that you need to give yourself 20-30 interviews to fine-tune your process and system. Don't look for new business after just a few interviews; this is a long-term strategy. But believe me, it will pay off for you! It took over 40 interviews before I started seeing some traction and momentum from the benefit of interviewing people on my radio show. It is something that is an excellent networking opportunity. It's a fantastic pre-sales opportunity. It's an incredible Authority Positioning and Authority Selling™ opportunity for you. Make sure that you're doing it, and doing it consistently.

Think about interviewing an Authority, where else could you have secured twenty minutes of time with someone at their level? Even when you bring a guest on your show to interview who may not be well-known, it is a very worthwhile investment of your time because they may be someone who you would like to do business with or work toward developing a strategic alliance. After the interview, ask if they can think of someone they would recommend you interviewing. This is a powerful step to do after every single interview because many times they will think of a name right then and you can ask if they could introduce you.

AUTHORITY SELLING™ EXECUTION TIP:
When you get a nice list of Influencers that you have interviewed on your podcast, offer limited slots up for your high-value sales prospects to come on your show. This gives them an incredible opportunity to begin building their own Authority, and it also is a great positioning session when you are interviewing them. Afterward, getting a sales meeting scheduled is a done deal!

After the interview has been published for a while, connect with them to see if you can do a follow-up interview. Make a note in your CRM system that summarizes what you talked about, and chances are, if you did a good job in the first interview, they'll give you another one.

Now that you have interviews down pat, you can begin to work on becoming an interview guest yourself. Many of your guests will have their own podcast or radio show, and you can ask to come on their program. Being interviewed helps you frame yourself as an Expert and an Authority with a significant amount of credibility from the position of speaking specifically about your area of expertise at length. Since your interviewer will also share your interview content, it helps you extend your reach.

When someone interviews you, you'll also get great content to use on your website, online and offline.

Once you start doing interviews and positioning yourself as an Expert, it leads to more interviews that you can do because you're going to use them as a sales tool to get on other podcasts and radio shows. Now the Media or Press page on your website is growing pretty quickly with quality content. These are wonderful ways that help you stay in control of the story that is being told about you online.

Although there will be individuals who contact you for interviews, you should also be proactive in going out and finding good interview opportunities. You can do a Google search on getting booked on podcast and radio shows. There are some services that are free, some that are low cost, and some are higher cost services, where they will book you on radio shows and podcasts and do all the work for you. In your local area, look at the local AM radio stations or local smaller FM radio stations; if you explain who you are, your expertise, and what value you bring to their audience, you may find that you can easily get on terrestrial stations as well.

One resource that can help you get seen and get some media mentions is Help a Reporter Out (HARO). It's a news sourcing service that connects Experts to journalists. When a journalist needs an Expert on a given topic, they can put in a query on HARO. As a source, you can search for journalists looking for an Expert in your field. It's a very, very popular service for you to get some media mentions.

As you start your interview journey, keep in mind the overall goal of the process; become the Educator and Advocate for your target audience in a sincere and genuine way. This builds your Authority Positioning status like nothing else.

AUTHORITY SELLING™ ACTION GUIDE:

List your primary goals for using interviews with
industry Influencers in your business marketing.

_____

_____

_____

_____

_____

_____

_____

_____

_____

_____

_____

_____

_____

What are the results you would like to see when you conduct interviews with key Influencers, strategic alliances and prospects in your industry?

_____

_____

_____

_____

_____

_____

_____

_____

_____

_____

_____

_____

_____

_____

_____

_____

_____

_____

Where are places you can reach these Influencers?

_____

_____

_____

_____

_____

_____

_____

_____

_____

_____

_____

_____

_____

_____

_____

_____

Authority Selling™ 3-Steps to Success:

Implementation Guide

Are you ready to start creating and amplifying your Authority Positioning and Influence? When you have your Authority Positioning Portfolio™, you have a powerful tool that will quickly help you persuade your prospects without being "pushy."

Use your Portfolio as an effective strategy for attracting high-paying clients & outselling your competition even if you feel you are a "Sales Introvert"!

You must develop your:

1. **Authority Positioning Platform**

What is your Competitive Advantage or Unique Selling Proposition (USP)?

2. **Authority Positioning Portfolio™**

What assets do you have currently and will be working on building? Interviews, media mentions, client testimonials & books.

3. **Authority Selling™ Process**

The structure that you and your Team will use to deliver your Authority Positioning Portfolio™. This should be an email template saved or the physical package created with multiple copies on-hand ready to be sent out.

Once you have your Authority Positioning Portfolio™, you are ready to begin using it everywhere you can! Think about how it can open doors to get interviewed on podcasts and radio shows or to be able to get quality guests on your show! What about when you go out to a networking meeting? What a great follow-up tool!

Imagine getting ready for a sales meeting with a prospect you have been working on landing for months. You realize that this sale would make-or-break your quarterly numbers. You finally have the meeting set with their Management Team for next week.

What if you sent each of them an overnight package with a professional cover letter intro expressing how the upcoming meeting will lay out your plan for their success, but in the package, you also include your Authority Portfolio:

o   Color copies of media mentions you have been featured in

o   Testimonials and Reviews from your raving fan clients.

o   Flash drive or Video Brochure with 2-3 radio and podcast interviews you have conducted as well as interviewing Influencers in their industry that they will recognize.

o   A copy of your Amazon bestselling book with a professional color glossy cover featuring your name and picture and the title describes your solution that you provide to customers or companies that have similar problems

When this package is delivered a few days before your presentation, and then you arrive for the meeting, are you perceived differently than your competitor that they are also meeting with that week?

This Authority Positioning Portfolio™ can also be delivered electronically for the sales presentations that are not as high-profile. You can set each of those items up on a page on your website with links to each item and send the sales prospect the link in advance of your meeting. Keep in mind; this is NOT a mass-marketing technique. The real power is to "Open More Doors to Close More Business."

So whether you use it to get the meeting in the first place, or to "Pre-Frame" your presentation before you arrive, or even as a "drop the mic" moment to leave behind after the presentation…you will succeed with this Authority Selling™ approach!

There you have it. The Authority Selling™ System thoroughly explained in this step-by-step process. Everything you need to apply in your business and use it for attracting high-paying clients & outselling your competition.

My vision is that every Entrepreneur and sales team in the world will someday have an Authority Selling™ Portfolio and use it to skyrocket sales. And my mission is to make sure that this powerful system is within reach no matter the size of the organization; from the single entrepreneur working from home to the Fortune 5000 organizations looking to take their business to the next level.

Where do you go from here? Well, it's like the saying "Knowledge is Power"; actually Knowledge is only POTENTIAL power, the real power comes in implementing and executing!

Go back through the book and make some extra notes, study the Execution Tips, complete the Action Guide and make a plan of action to build your Authority Selling™ Portfolio and implement The Authority Selling™ System in your business.

You've got everything you need to take action. The only question is this: Are you willing to get to work?

Because now is the time! For the best way to move forward, you can choose to implement the ideas and strategies presented in this book and do-it-yourself. Get started today and put them in action, you'll feel great seeing progress in your marketing and promotions!

I would like to give you some guidance here on additional options:

Option 1: Do nothing at all

Please don't let this book be just another business book you read so that you can check it off of your list!

Option 2: Work with someone you find online

The strategies in this book are not new; you can find service providers to work with for your projects. I would caution you to make sure that they have a track record themselves of building and promoting their Authority!

Option 3: Work with my team and me to build your Authority Selling™ Portfolio

If you'd like to know your Authority Positioning Portfolio™ is being done right, have our Team do all the work for you from the strategy foundation to the tactics of your Expert interview, transcription into your book, formatting for Kindle and paperback and professional book cover creation.

You can find out how to work with us by visiting:

www.MarketingHuddle.com

Whatever you decide, the most important thing is to take action while this is on your mind, it is so rewarding to see action pay off!

Take a small step today, another step tomorrow and before you know it, you'll be well on your way to implementing the Authority Selling™ System in your business!

Made in the USA
Columbia, SC
21 June 2017